W0115567

No Margin 4 Error

Alfredo Barrios Sr.

ISBN (Print Edition): 978-1-54396-349-6

ISBN (eBook Edition): 978-1-54396-349-6

© 2019. All rights reserved. No part of this publication may be reproduced, distributed, or transmitted in any form or by any means, including photocopying, recording, or other electronic or mechanical methods, without the prior written permission of the publisher, except in the case of brief quotations embodied in critical reviews and certain other noncommercial uses permitted by copyright law.

NO MARGIN 4 ERROR

ALFREDO BARRIOS SR.

TABLE OF CONTENTS

CHAPTER 1
YOUNG HUSTLER

At the age of 15, I experienced what it felt like to be in a jail cell. I was sentenced to 90 days in juvenile camp for possession of narcotics on school grounds. I was shooting dice in the bathroom with a few other young hustlers when the school narc walked in on us. We were escorted to the principal's office and asked to empty out our pockets. Unfortunately, when I turned my jacket pockets inside out, a piece of white rock flew onto the desk of the principle. As the principle was examining the rock (we both knew what it was), I tried to snatch it away from his hands, but unfortunately, I swung and missed.

Once released from camp, I met a girl from the neighborhood, and we developed a relationship that would produce a son—we were kids having kids. A good friend of the family helped me land a job in a warehouse, but I was let go after a few weeks because I was not 18 years of age at the time. I had choices to make, and school did not seem to be one of them. I had a choice between getting a minimum wage job and going out on the streets and hustle. The latter would mean jeopardizing my freedom and the start of a life of incarceration. My family had the dope house hustle, serving rock cocaine during the "Cavy" epidemic. I would wake up in the mornings to go to school and I would see the piles of cash next to my sleeping brother who was up all-night hustling. I wanted to get money too. I was a kid who was heading in the wrong direction, blinded by the illusion of the come up and everything that comes along with it. Growing up in the 80's, in a community that was plagued with gangs, drugs, and violence, every teenager had to make choices to avoid the pain that the street life can cause. Throughout my youth, it seemed like I was destined for nothing but failure due to my negative outlook in solving issues.

I remember the day my son was born. I was ecstatic. It was a Friday night and my high school had a football game that evening. I went there with cigars and passed them out to some of the fellas, as if this was a normal tradition for a teenage father. A few weeks later, on the day he was circumcised, he was crying late into the night and woke-up his mom and my sisters. My oldest sister Juanita thought she heard my cousins outside speaking, so she opened the front door to let them in, but two strangers with guns pointed at her face greeted her. She lost her voice as one of the gunmen pulled the trigger, but the gun jammed and they both ran off. My brother and I went looking for these individuals in the car around the neighborhood, and the only thing we had in mind was to cancel their birthday.

Our street was known as a hangout for many, and we encountered enemies for various reasons. I recall having our house shot at so many times that it became normal to hit the ground until you could hear the car taking off and try to see who it was in order to retaliate. I still remember hearing my mother crying and praying. The police would come out as protocol, but they knew they were not going to get any information from us. It was the same police from the same police department that I felt were disrespecting our property while looking for drugs and weapons during their early morning raids. I also remember being arrested for spitting on the sidewalk once and choked by officers in the back of a police car. Later, inside a holding cell next to mine, I heard my brother get beaten by several officers. As you can imagine, my outlook toward police officers was negative.

Looking back on the lifestyle we lived, selling drugs and being the neighborhood's fireworks party at any given moment, was disrespectful to our community, and I now understand. I have a different perspective toward law enforcement—one of gratitude today. We were raised by two respectful parents who managed to work hard and provide for a family of seven, but the fast life seemed more interesting to us. My parents instilled in us the value of keeping our word, respect, and to always defend ourselves. Being a police officer is not an easy job today as some injustices have caused broken trust amongst communities throughout our country. I believe the only way to build trust amongst law enforcement and communities is to work together by creating opportunities for our youth before gangs and negative influences pulls them into the false promises of street glamour.

When I turned 16, the worst thing that could happen, happened. My father was shot and killed. If I had any dreams that were positive, they all disappeared and I no longer had a care in the world. All I wanted was revenge. My father was a hard worker—well respected—and he did not deserve to lose his life the way that he did. My mother was on a 22-hour road trip to Mexico the day before his death, and the moment she arrived there she had to turn around since she received the news of her husband being murdered! I was heartbroken to see my father lying motionlessly on the ground, surrounded by a pool of blood. All I could think of was that it was my fault for delaying, for whatever excuse I gave not to go with him and my mother to Mexico.

I recall that Sunday vividly. The morning started off with a baseball game that my two brothers and I played every Sunday. After the game, we returned to the dope house my brothers had and Joseph brought in some food to eat. Pops was with us eating and telling us that it was time for my mother and him to go live in Mexico. My father was going to leave the following week and seemed excited to return to his homeland and building on the land they'd purchased to live out their lives. About an hour later, I left and so did my older brother. Pops went back out to the neighbor's house and was enjoying a Sunday afternoon with his friends having a beer. I arrived at my sister's home in Lynwood to the phone ringing. I answered and was informed that there was a shooting in front of my brother's house. I ran into my car and took every light no matter the color back to Long Beach. As I arrived, I saw my older brother waiting for me with bad news. I could hear him saying, "Pops is gone." I tried to go see my father lying on the concrete, but the police did not allow me, in order to conduct their investigation. I was in disbelief. I recall running up the street and around the blocks kicking in someone's fence from the anger I had, hoping that when I returned to the scene of the crime my father was still alive. When I did return, my oldest sister was there and broken in tears. My brother and I jumped into the Monte Carlo without any weapons and drove to where we knew we would someday return the pain we felt. Revenge was imminent.

CHAPTER 2
ON THE RUN

Eight months had gone by since the murder of my father. I was in a 1973 Monte Carlo with my son and being pursued by the police. I knew I was wanted for a shooting because the night of the incident the victim's brother was inside the police car in front of the location where I was living at the time, giving them my name. I had made a negative choice from the loss of my father as I blocked out anything else but the thoughts of revenge.

A few weeks later on Christmas day, I was with my son and his mother when I was arrested for five counts of attempted murder. I tried to get away, but once the helicopter is on you, you are done. My one-year old son is the reason why I did not pursue a high-speed chase. I cannot say the thought of trying to escape the squad cars and helicopter did not enter my mind, but I had to face the music because the safety of my son and his mother were my priority. I had just turned 17 years old, and it was time deal with the consequences. I was arrested and taken to juvenile hall and tried as an adult to face charges on five counts of attempted murder. Every court date, I would be taken from juvenile hall early in the morning to the Men's County Jail and placed in the special cages the bus had adapting to a new world that one must be vigilant at all times. I soon realized that

I did not have control of my freedom and transform my mentality to survive in order to retain freedom someday again. I was facing a sentence of 15 years to life. I knew that I would be heading to prison, being tested coming in to the juvenile system as every other teen and went into the cell a few times with individuals who just didn't like my program. I also had physical encounters with staff, but never filed grievances afterwards keeping my mouth shut, which worked to my benefits throughout my time at the halls.

The guys who were shot were from the gang that was involved in shooting my father, except for one individual. I must give him the utmost respect. He was at the wrong place at the wrong time but kept it the way the game was intended during court proceedings. The district attorney brought in all the victims to court to testify against me. They also wanted to testify against my older brother who was not involved with the shooting but was implicated out of fear from the victims. First, the witnesses said under oath that I was the shooter, and then they change their story and said my brother was. When I saw these guys in the courtroom, all I could do was laugh at them because it showed their true character. They wanted to play the gun game but could not handle it when the rabbit had the gun. They showed up to the preliminary hearing wearing white t-shirts and pants sagging staring at my brother and me as if they wanted to take flight. As the hearing continued, my attorney caught them in a lie. The DA tried to clean their lie up as best as possible, but that damage their case. We were facing a life sentence and after the hearing our attorneys sat with us to discuss a plea bargain of three years, if we plead guilty to assault with a deadly weapon.

I wanted to go to trial and beat the case especially since I knew my brother was innocent, but he made me take the deal. I remember sitting in the attorney room and he said that if we lost, we would receive a life sentence. We accepted the deal and one year later, I was free. I was sent to California Youth Authority for a 90-day observation, but I asked the judge to send me to prison when I returned to court. I was 18 and knew the asinine games that were played in youth authority would cause me to max out as they called it, and back then it could have been until you turned 25 years old. Going to prison I would be home in less than one year, so I took that route. Joe still had a few more years to serve since he had taken another deal also in a different courtroom for another case that he was not involved with either, but his reputation as a shooter pursued him.

I was never a hard-core gangster, just a young hustler. I carried a pair of dice in my pocket looking to shoot for a dollar every day or pitching quarters on the way to school "playing get like me" with friends. Being late for 1st period and continuing gambling at school during lunch in the restroom shooting dice. I was motivated to the fast life seeing my family get it, and though it was the wrong way, it was intriguing. One thing that I learned from my family growing up was that if you play the gun game, expect others to be playing as well. We understood the consequences that came with our actions, but keeping our mouth shut about who shot at our home or even to testify in any case against anyone that may have been involved in my Father's murder we never cooperated in. My family was about hustling with a shooting touch, and with that street hustle comes envy. The game was and is a dirty one with the more you make, the more individuals will hate you. If you are not prepared to spend the rest of your life in prison for the cause of the game, or lose your life, then you should find another passion fast. After losing my father I was prepared to lose my life and accept a life sentence in prison for vengeance, but not for some street that we grew up on. I was taught to respect everyone, but also to not be afraid of losing my release date.

I recall my brother and me being escorted inside the attorney room at the courthouse. We were not cuffed and without any leg irons as we entered to speak with our attorneys. Inside was an individual with leg irons and cuffed around his waist and apparently knew my brother, and from the tension, I sensed that he was an enemy, and I was correct. This individual was being charged with the murder of my father...I was waiting on my brother to make a move and when he did not after like one second, he told me that we could stomped this individual out, but we would lose respect from many because he was cuffed up. Perhaps it would have been a coward move to react out of anger and frustration by beating this individual badly, but we were raised to be fair. The bailiff's must have known something because they came and took him out within minutes. I respect and understood my brother's reasons, and also the racial tension throughout the county jail of the aftermath.

Growing up in a gang-plagued community, I recall my brother and friends always hanging out and playing sports. When I was the youngest by five years or so, they were all in school together and our home had the doors open to them all with our parent's blessings. As the years went on and the friendships developed to family love, we were known as a Fam Bam that was about their hustle and willing to defend the street we were raised on. Our parents loved each one as their own making sure a taco was at least offered to them if they were hungry. One of the traits our parents had was that they embraced an individual no matter their nationality. Growing up in a diverse community, we did not see any color lines, developing close bonds with friends that were of different ethnicity. I met with people who disliked me, because of the street I grew up on during my incarceration, but I did not owe anyone an explanation. I was riding with survival and that meant trust no one...period. I was going to be respectful, but also demand it in return, and deal with any issues that came my way the best way I thought I could. No matter what ethnicity it was, I was going to defend myself if it meant stabbing someone to prove a point. The murder of my father and friends made me understand that I should not trust anyone, regardless of whom I considered a friend. I was ready to defend myself inside the prison system that I was headed to. Individuals that I thought were friends growing up were now rumored to be involved, and even tried to take my life and freedom. I had to be on a solo mind and let time take its course through the ride.

I was released December 16th, 1993 to a completely new war...

CHAPTER 3
TRUST NO ONE

In October of 1993, I was in Chuckwalla State Prison with a little over a month left before my release. I was watching the ten o' clock news and I just happened to see that there was a shooting in Long Beach which killed five people—four males and one pregnant female. Two of the individuals killed were like family as we had grown up together and live next door to one another. All victims were shot in the head. The day of the viewing more gunfire was shed at the cemetery. My oldest sister was pregnant at the time and had been hit with buckshot's and thank God she is doing well today with a goal-oriented son. When I was released, I was told so many different versions of who was involved. After a few weeks of being released I was in the front yard with my mother who was watering the lawn, when an individual drove by my home disrespecting the lives that were taken. A gunshot was heard, and the police came to our home looking for me as the shooter. I was on the run since I was on parole. This individual was shot and mentioned my name to the police as he went to the hospital. A couple of days later I was a sitting duck in front of a place I visited on the boulevard and was shot at close range seven to eight times. I was not hit but knew who did it. I was slipping and knew it, but I was not going to contact the police. Speaking with the law was frown upon. I was putting together in my mind how I would strike back but before I could, I was arrested for a parole violation.

During the time of my arrest, guns were found underneath my home, so I knew I was headed to Chino on a violation. I received a year parole violation and so did my brother in law since he was also on parole and at the home during the raid. During the year I was serving I thought about how individuals played the game. Many fronted how solid they were. I knew I wanted to make money once I had my freedom again and get as far away as possible from a lifestyle that had no bright promises, but I also knew that I did not want to return to prison and deal with prison drama. I had some visions and business ideas, but lack of funds was my excuse. I had to make choices fast and was introduced to inside jobs that were worth the risk I felt. This was going to be the way out I told myself, but God had other plans for me. I was making moves that involved making good money, but I was also jeopardizing my freedom and my family. I was arrested 10 months later during a job I was given by individuals that said big money was inside of a home. A partner and I did the job and I was caught during a foot chase. I had no way out and was surrounded by police officers as I was hiding under a dark area at a park. I could see an officer running my way with her gun out as I jumped up without any thought; this scared the officer and she was yelling at me to get down—shaking with her gun drawn. Looking back at that evening and moment now, I am grateful that she did not shoot me.

I knew life was going to change and all I could think of was failing my son. I had planted in my mind that this move was going to be the one in keeping my five-year-old son far away from the neighborhood I had grown up in. I did not want him to experience the shootings or raids by police officers that our family met. I had already made the move to Moreno Valley, and I was working on building my own family away in an unfamiliar environment. I kept feeding myself that we were going to flip the money and keep building after this move, which meant that I was not allowing my mind to open to positive opportunities. I was willing to risk it all and lost.

My partner was never caught nor mentioned, and I was offered a deal of 14 years with 85% or face the 39 years that the DAwas going to pursue if convicted. I knew I would be convicted since the victims were at every court appearance. I am not proud of my actions as a youth and young adult, nor can I erase the memory of that day for the victims that I caused trauma too. I have prayed and prayed for forgiveness and apologize to my victims. God will be the true judge and juror upon my resting period.

When I took this deal, I was 22 years old and the year was 1996. I gave up my freedom and gave up any opportunity to raise my son. My release date was in 2007 and that seemed so far away. Every day I kept telling myself that the laws would change and that the over-crowding would result in advance release. I wrote to my son as much as possible and thanked his grandmother for keeping me updated with him. He was growing up in the same neighborhood I did, and I prayed that he would make wiser choices as he became a young teenager. I wish to pay my respects for his mother, as she did the best to secure a roof over his head and food on the table.

I was sentence to 14 years with 85% and headed back to prison. After my 90 orientation inside the intake prison, I was sent to another prison in San Luis Obispo. This prison was known for housing dropouts from prison gangs, homosexuals and there were a lot of snitches—and I did not want a part of it. CMC was mellow—I could relax and do my time and not worry about anything, but I was not comfortable with eating on the same tables with child molesters and having correctional officers talk badly. The word on this prison was that if you stayed in this prison for longer than 90 days, you were considered trash to rest of the prison population throughout the system. I knew what the consequences were going to be for my actions, but I figured I was still incarcerated no matter where they send me. I had to get out of this place and the only way to do so was to get into one fight and I would be on my way to another prison.

I had been in prison before but not for long, three years was the most time I had served but this time it was going to be for a while. I had a brief stay at San Luis Obispo, as I am in the hole for an altercation with another individual waiting on a bus ride, I could view outside through a window into the prison yard and see that most inmates just wanted to serve their time without any problems but were not to be trusted. As I watched daily out the window waiting for the process of being transferred, I thought about my current situation. I was a young 22-year-old adult with more than 10 years of prison time I owed the state of California. I had to remind myself that I was fortunate to have a release date. I could hear some of the other men on the tier speaking at night to their neighbors about level four prison yards. They made it sound scary. The write-up I received from the altercation caused my points to go up to a level four status. I was going to have a free ride to another prison someplace, but now I it would be to the maximum-security level four yard. All I kept hearing was to get your knife ready. I remember telling myself if I ever get the opportunity again to be free, I am going to make the best with it and enjoy every day that I can...I had to snap out of that dream and start preparing myself mentally and physically for the next step—the infamous level four yard.

CHAPTER 4
THE LEARNING CENTER

During my stay in the "hole" as they called it, I received my transfer papers going to some prison that housed some of the most violent convicts with riots and stabbings occurring frequently. Fistfights were not common at all, but stabbings were the method of obligation to solve disputes. I spent 90 days in the hole waiting on the bus schedule to pick me up. As I arrived at my new location, my body was shivering. After all the processing was done, I was taken to a cell around 1:30 am. A tray slot open and the lights to the cell came on. The inmate inside had to place his hands through the tray slot and cuff up for the cell to open. After the door shut, we both repeated the process again of our hands through the slot, but this time to be un-cuff.

My cellmate was a guy, who little bit older than me with a life sentence for murder. We introduce ourselves and one of the first things he did was take out a yellow form called a 128 Chrono—your license to stay on the yard. This form had all your convictions, affiliation, and if there were anything negative on my 128, it would be his obligation to stab me and get me off the yard. He asked me respectfully if I had my form with me, so he could feel comfortable sleeping in a cell with someone he knew passed the background check. This goes throughout the universal system including County Jails My paperwork passed, and the learning process began. The first lesson learned was that I no longer had a release date. My brother in law's words started to hit me. This is the place he was referring to when he described prison. His advice along with my older brother's and the street knowledge that I had learned as a kid was the way I survived the system. I recall my brother telling me that the moment I felt any negative vibe from someone, if they came within reaching distance from me, was to take off on the spot. I also was taught from my brother in law, who was more like my real brother, to be prepared and willing to give up my release date for survival. He said that I should have to make a jailhouse weapon and be prepared to use it, but just as the street rule applies about carrying a gun, the same concept applies with a jailhouse weapon inside. Do not carry one if you are only fronting to put fear in someone because you will be tested and do not fail that test.

I witness men being stabbed—shot by the gunner in the tower—and killed. I learned to keep quiet and not ask questions about who is doing what because when you ask about something regarding jailhouse politics, you are raising your hand to take care of issues. Viewing individuals being stabbed by the same individuals they walked the track with and called their homies made me understand the politics inside. I did not want any of part them and used common sense to stay away from drama and get creative to grow mentally. I was just a visitor in the prison system, not a lifer. Here you had men who are serving life sentences without the possibility of parole and others with over 50 years to serve that just want to live out their life with solid individuals in their world. They do not want rapist, Chester's, snitches, or dead weights taking up a bed for a solid one in waiting. These are the men that are about that life and will do whatever it takes to support and have these policies respected. They are willing to die on site for a cause that demands respect, power, and obedience.

Convicts run the system inside, the guards just have the keys to open doors. Prison politics is so much like our political politics in which there is a structure of well-educated individuals working on policies who will generate income for their own agendas. I learned to have the utmost respect for individuals who take the idle time in their lives and put it to good used to prepare for the opportunity of freedom someday. If you are not mentally and emotionally strong, you will not survive. The sharks will cajole you and swallow you alive. Rising early in the morning to pray and meditate, reading, writing and drawing, was a program I adapted with to have the day go by without my mind wandering on the negative side. My drawing skills were in beginner's mode, but taking advantage of lock-downs of months at a time to learn a new hustle. I tried not to bother family at all in regard to any financial help, as it was my own mistakes that sent me to prison. When I would receive a package or funds from siblings or anyone, I was grateful and appreciative. One thing that kept me strong was my Faith in God to keep fighting, which reminded me daily that I would make it out to the free world one last time. I stayed at this prison for 18-months before receiving a special visit from two individuals that would soon test my strength.

CHAPTER 5

FIGHTING 4 FREEDOM

Four years had passed by since receiving a 14-year term. I was told I had an attorney visit and escorted to the visiting room where I met with two detectives from Long Beach California. The moment I walked into the visiting room and asked to see their badges, "Homicide Division" I got up and asked to be escorted back to my yard. I knew it was not good as I had outstanding debts to be paid. These detectives were upset with me because they came from far away to speak with me, and I had no time for them. They even had a bet amongst themselves that I would or wouldn't speak with them about their case. Good cop bad cop game. I told them to go enjoy the infamous Mustang Ranch (brothel) on taxpayer funds. They were not my friends, nor did they have my best interest. They wanted me to talk about a murder case that they were investigating and give them any information that would help them convict others or myself. Two weeks later, I was on a bus being taken back to L.A. County Jail to face murder charges with special circumstances carrying capital punishment.

I recall my attorney visiting me at the LA county jail and asking me questions for the death penalty committee. He asked me about my religious beliefs and reasons why I should not be sentence to death if found guilty on all charges. I told him that I would prefer the death penalty rather than serving the rest of my life in prison if convicted, and the reason for that was that I would get a closer look at all my appeals thoroughly before being put to death by lethal injection. If it was God's will that I be put to death due to my mistakes in life, then I had to accept it, but not without a fight. Somehow, the death penalty committee ruled that the maximum punishment would be the (LWOP) life without parole if convicted. I began to value what many of us take for granted. Freedom! My release date of 2007 no longer existed, and the only way I could regain that date was to be acquitted by a jury of my peers or my case being dismissed by the presiding judge. I was not going to accept any plea deals on these charges and was eager to get into the ring for the fight of my lifetime. I was not accepting in my mind or out of my mouth a life sentence during the court proceedings. I needed this fight to grow mentally, to discover my passion in life, and to believe in Divine Faith.

I had a co-defendant at the time, but we manage to have our cases separated for trial since it was his statements that implicated me. He had been arrested for gun charges and was release on a special deal in exchange to help the police with unsolved murders. During one of his visits to the police department, there was a video tape recording of all the questions being asked. He described murder scenes that took place during the time that I had my freedom and mentioned my name. He said he had heard I was involved and somehow, then broke down and mention he was a part of it. By him saying that after questioning was over, handcuffs were placed on him and he was charged with murder. He was not offer immunity for his testimony and now was facing the death penalty as well. This was someone whom I considered more than just a friend; he was family. I remember seeing him for the first time and he could not look me in the eye. I knew that he had given a statement to the police about me, but his statement was not admissible in trial unless he was willing to say the same in front of a jury. I held my composure and told him it was alright. We were never in the same holding cell as he had to be alone always due to his request of needing protection. He was being housed in the County Jail also but secluded in the protective custody section of the jail. No one on the main line likes a snitch and other inmates would speak badly to him during the ride back to county jail after court. No other inmates could get to him because he was in a small cage locked away during the bus ride, but they called him names and spit or even pissed on him and vise- versa. My codefendant was known to throw piss or spit at those who mocked him. I tried to always keep a level of respect verbally with him during every encounter we had because even though his testimony could keep me away from ever knowing what freedom felt like again, his silence could also help.

I was skeptical to be on the same bus ride with him and felt the DA was setting me up the times when we did share a ride back to county jail. I was not a big shot inside, but I gave every man the respect that I wanted in return. Fighting Murder Charges helped with my request to some of the inmates that knew about my codefendant, if they could please not spit or speak badly to him while I was on the bus with him. I wanted him to feel that at least for the bus ride back to County Jail, the ride would be peaceful and we both could enjoy seeing the bridge on Atresia above the 710 freeway with visions of walking over it freely again. I think he knew he would never drive nor walk across that bridge again, but he also knew it was his own mouth that took away that chance. He had earned his respect and ruined his image by not understanding the consequences from his choices. The thought of being able to handle prison for the rest of your life is different from the reality. Not everyone can handle prison time or to be isolated in a cell for 24 hour a day inside the county jail, not knowing if it's day or night outside causing many inmates mental issues and suicidal thoughts.

My codefendant received his verdict the same day his trial concluded. He was found guilty on all charges and would be receiving a LWOP sentence. His sentence date was schedule and the prosecution needed his statement to convict me. He mentioned to me on the bus that he would not get on the stand and testify against me no matter what, and that the detectives had lied to him during questioning about me. They told him I had already made statements about his involvement in the case, so he felt he would do the same. I had copies of all paperwork of the entire case and never did I answer or wanted to know anything about this case from detectives. Tape recordings of him during interview from detectives were more than enough to convict him. He also had all paperwork and apologizes to me for his careless mistake that would cost him his freedom and life.

During the first trial, he was brought in to give his testimony to the jury and the only thing he said was that he wanted to go back to his cell. He did not have anything else to say. His statement that he gave to detectives could not be used against me and that was a major blow to the prosecution's case. I had never actually been through a jury trial and the scariest part is the deliberation process. When your freedom is in the hands of 12 strangers, all you can do is pray for strength and accept the verdict. I had heard all the horror stories of juries that many just want to deliver a verdict the same day because they do not get paid for their time accordingly. Choosing my first jury with my attorney was an experience I would never forget. We had the right to dismiss any protential jurors but had to strategize because we had a limit to dismiss. It was like a chess match between the district attorney and my attorney. When we finally decided on the jury, it was time to fight and hold on to faith, understanding that God would be the ruler.

My attorney was an older Caucasian man that lived in Malibu, whom my family had used on prior occasions dating back to the days of the fast life. He was losing his touch and my level of trust in him was uncertain. During some court hearings, I would look over to him and see his eyes closed as if he was napping. He said he was thinking but I swear I could hear a snore or two. After my first trial ended and the case was handed over to the jury, I remember sitting in the court tanks waiting for a verdict with so many different thoughts in my head. That was the most challenging time of my life. I did not want a quick decision, which would have assured a guilty verdict, and I did not want it to take a week, as the feeling in my stomach was unpleasant. After the first full day of waiting, there was no verdict. The next day we did it all over again and no decision. I had been seeing my bailiff come in and out of the tanks calling out other inmates for court, but every time I saw her, I swear chills would occur. Then the third day arrived and just before lunch my bailiff calls my name. She said she did not know the verdict but to this day, I believe they know before us. I change into my street clothes that were provided from my brother Ish, transforming into a young man who looked and felt free. Both sides gave it their best shot and the verdict was now on paper to be read out load by the court clerk. As I walked into the courtroom and was seated, next to me was the lead detective in the case with the district attorney. I glance at my left and he was staring at me without a blink. He played the good cop role when he and his partner flew out to visit me about this case. I stared back to try and figured out if I could read the verdict through his eyes, as if to say I got you, you will spend the rest of your life in prison, but I could not see a smirk on his face. My bailiff tried to come and make me look the other way, but what were they going to do to me. I was already incarcerated and if I were found guilty, I would have preferred to go back to the county jail and be in the hole all alone. This is a place where men can cry and have a peace of mind all alone. Every man sheds a tear from time to time, and there is nothing wrong with that. Incarceration will break down the biggest, the toughest, and the most prideful. The moment the verdict was about to be read, my heart began to pound 10 times faster. Nine jurors found me guilty and three were undecided, resulting in a hung jury. The case was dismissed, but refilled immediately.

CHAPTER 6
ROUND 2...

The year was 2000, the year that the world was going to end supposedly. I could only enjoy all the festivities in my mind and convince myself that my time will come to be a part of the joy that the free world was experiencing. Telling myself not to give up as the first trial only gave me hope and appreciation for freedom. They say that everything happens for a reason, good or bad. It is up to us to dissect and direct our path from it. I was at a prison where if I had stayed another year, I would have lost my release date by defending myself to the best of my ability with a jail house weapon. There were individuals on the same yard who were considered enemies from the streets but due to lock downs the opportunities to cross path did not allow us. Though I was headed back to court to face new charges that would wipe away the reality of freedom if convicted, I viewed this with a positive mindset to find the passion within me. Too many lockdowns would not allow for consistent vocational programs flow due to the safety of the institution, and I was happy to get away from an environment that violence was inevitable.

I had to be mindful every day, telling myself that this will be the biggest test of my life. That if I was going to be on a level four yard ever again, it would be with a life sentence and nothing to lose. I was going through all the steps once again to start the second trial of the case I was being charged with MURDER!

I had received news that my older brother was arrested and in the county jail. I had been in the county jail for over a year and had a little pull with some of the officers in the building since they respected how I ran my program and was not some knuckle head. I had asked one of the officers if they could look my brother up and bring him to the same location that I was at if possible. Joe was facing a lot of time due to his third strike and knew if I lost my case, I would never get an opportunity to see him again perhaps. A few weeks later, my brother shows up in the same pod I was housed. It felt good knowing that no matter what, I had one person there with me who would never turn on me and had my back to the fullest as I would have his. Joe had been arrested for five pounds of marijuana hustling to fuel his visions as an entrepreneur. Though his methods to obtain capital were not legit, his heart was solid to build for his family. As I was going back and forth with my second trial, he was a powerful influence in giving me positive encouragement.

Being housed at one location for over a year fighting for my life, I had the privilege to take part in weekly Bible Studies from Pastor's that volunteered their time which always gave a sense of hope afterwards for all the inmates. I knew God was working with me slowly and teaching me how to forgive. I looked forward to Sunday morning church inside the pods we were housed in every week just to take part in the singing of "This Little Light of Mine." Each pod house a total of 20 men or so who were all fighting a case involving serious time. Not all the men took part of the services as they wanted to stay in bed on a Sunday morning, but I needed my weekly fix. I was on a schedule of getting up early every day no matter what day it was. I could see and feel the transformation inside of me during this time of my life. Something the pastor or a visitor with the group would say would give me strength through the days to come. I was grateful for their prayers as they asked God to be the true juror and judge during my trials.

During my second trial, we picked a different jury and my attorney was better prepared than the first trial. I also became my own attorney as I had questions for him to ask the witnesses and had reviewed all my files repeatedly. I had highlighted what I believe witnesses had contradicted themselves with from the police reports to the trial transcripts. I also read law books that pertained to my case to learn about technicalities. My codefendant was brought in again to testify during my second trial, and when put on the stand he said the same thing as the first trial. All he wanted was to return to his cell again. He was already found guilty of murder and was never going to experience true freedom. On the bus drive back to County Jail my codefendant sticks his fingers out through the gap in cage he was sitting in, and we lock our fingers together as we both knew this would be the final time we would see each other.

During the trial as I was placed into a holding cell for a 10-minute break, I had a feeling of being cold and shivers passing all over my body. Perhaps because I was afraid of the unknown outcome, but I fell to my knees and said a prayer. I said, "God, if you know that I will hurt someone again or go out into the free world to corrupt young minds, then keep me here for the rest of my life...but if you know that through my testimony, I can reach our youth to help them avoid making the same mistakes that I made, then I welcome the opportunity to be set free as per your will." The second trial was now over, and the case was handed to the jury. I had a new judge presiding over the case and who had a reputation of being one of the strictest. I had to deal with the deliberation phase all over again.

My heart pumping faster than normal just like in the previous trial. I had no appetite through it all, and I had to remain calm respecting the outcome. Hope for the best, prepare for the worst mindset. That is how I felt. The jury deliberated for three days again as the bailiff handed me my street clothes to change into, (what a good feeling that was) I step inside the courtroom to learn my fate.

As the verdict was read out, I was numbed for a second. I could not believe this case was over and no more refiling. My attorney's grin displayed excitement and disbelief all in one. After two years of fighting to regain my release date, I was thankful for the outcome. I nodded and thank each juror as to say thank you for their time and for letting God be the one that will give his judgment over these charges. The jury could not reach a verdict on the murder charges but did find me not guilty on two other counts that were the premise of their case. The judge dismissed the case with prejudice, meaning that this case could no longer be refilled. He said that there would not be a jury in the world that would acquit me on the charges of murder, but also not one that would convict me. It would be a waste of taxpayer's money.

A few days after the case ended, I was back at the county jail when one of the deputies mentioned that someone took their own life at the Men's Central Jail the night before. This inmate returned form court in Long Beach and must have received unwelcome news. The inmate was my co-defendant as he made the decision to end his life rather than to man up. Those thoughts never entered my mind no matter the outcome. If I had been convicted on the charges, my plan was to make someone an example to respect my space and let me do me. I knew that I would need some time in the hole alone for the first few years, as I would need time to accept a life sentence. Learning to deal with the emotional pain in solitary until being mentally prepared to cope with the general population. I am grateful for the outcome never forgetting my prayer to God to be used in reaching our youth.

I do not hold any grudges with the detectives involved with the case, or the witnesses that came forth knowing they were being coach to testify. This case had not only opened my eyes to see life in a new perspective, but also my heart to give back in ways that my story may help someone from experiencing a reality of never having their freedom again. I was given my release date back, with seven years to serve before I could step on soil of freedom. It was time to focus and prepare a roadmap to my future.

CHAPTER 7
BUS RIDES

After getting to know the young men who received a life sentence or were also fighting for their lives during my trials, the hunger to reach out to our youth was growing inside my heart. Going through two trials where the penalty of a life sentence was on the line, I had a newfound empathy for them. I would tell them to pray and build a personal relationship with their God and to keep fighting. These youngsters did not know the reality of level four prison yard that awaited them but had heard of them through horror stories that other inmates had told them. I tried to speak and encourage those who would listen to not give up. Some would portray a tough guy image and think the "cause" was worth it all. Putting in work for their gang cost them the opportunity to be a part of society. Street gangs in our communities have taken away many young men and women from an opportunity to live their true dreams to living a reality of turmoil.

I had seven years left to serve on my 14-year sentence. In fact, I needed those years to mature and prepare for life outside the walls. I was a kid when I entered the system and had so much to learn if I wanted to be an asset. After the trials ended, I was sent to Delano State prison reception center awaiting to be transferred to the same level four prison I before my trials. I had been away for two years fighting my case, which meant that my classification points dropped down. I went to a classification hearing 10 days after my arrival and was informed that my points dropped down close to a level two, which meant I was waiting on a bus ride to another prison. The prison was on lockdown during my wait with tensions boiling high. I prayed that we would stay on lockdown until it was time to leave as I did not want anything to impede my transfer. I had gained so much respect for freedom after experiencing both trials; I had learned to appreciate a second chance. In every prison institution that I was temporarily housed in, I learned from someone that passed along a message of hope. It was time to for my transfer to a program yard. Arriving at Tehachapi, you could feel the atmosphere was very different. The dayrooms were open to go inside them and watch TV or play cards. There was open yard to go out and workout or walk around. You had lifers here that had over 20 years in and waiting for a release date once the board finds them fit to re-enter society as well as inmates going home every day. It was rare to see or hear of anyone going home from a level four yard. The respect level among inmates was different as some men would break the ice with each other and later would be working with feelings. The officers also took advantage of inmates having release dates and speaking to us disrespectful at times or disrespecting our property. I was adapting to the change and was going to stay productive and away from any drama. There was more drama at the lower levels since dayrooms open and yard open all day and gave men the opportunity to find a reason to start up chaos. Many times, it was junkies owing money that would cause tensions to rise or some narrow-minded person that wanted to stir the pot.

The hustler in me came out the moment that I was given a clerk job in the kitchen. I did not want to bother family or anyone for store money, so I quickly found out that sugar was a goldmine inside. I had access to it and would bring out a few pounds daily stacking up on top rumens and hygiene. I had a locker full of goodies avoiding the chow hall and the drama of being treated as a child with your blues on and I.D. bull crap. Though it was prison, I was enjoying the sports program when jailhouse drama broke out right next to my bunk, and I fell into my defense mode. When a riot breaks out, you better be ready to defend yourself from all angles or you will be a victim. There are no rules in weapons. I had locks inside socks and canned foods inside pillowcases swung at me during incidents at other prisons. I ended back in the hole here and was awaiting transfer once again to another prison. One of the good things that came out of this transfer was that I was going to the same prison my brother was in. He had received a life sentence for five pounds of marijuana possession. He is the same brother that was with me during the trial that would change my visions and the start of appreciation for freedom. We ended up becoming cellmates for over a year before my points dropped, and I was being transferred once again.

Leaving was bitter-sweet because we did not know how long it will be before we would see each other again, but with two years left to serve on the prison term I was sentenced to, we both agreed that moving on to a lower level prison, I could begin to mentally prepare for my release. This prison had so much going on and lock downs were often. After being in cells for so many years without much of outside activities, I wanted to prepare mentally for my freedom creating a road map that will guide me to enjoy it. During the time we were cellmates, we were able to mourn the loss of our brother-in-law who died of kidney failures—a solid streetwise hustler, with a heart of gold. Losing someone is difficult to begin with, but when you are in prison and you get news of someone dying in your family, it is dreadful. We shared moments of his memory together and a held moment of silent for him. I didn't mind transferring much because I did not want to stay in a prison too long never having the opportunity to see what the free world looked like and becoming institutionalize. Bus rides were very therapeutic, as I got the chance to see what life outside of prison was like. Seeing people walking around without cuffs and free to enjoy a meal gave me hope in my own freedom. I knew my time was coming, but it was now time to focus on the reality of my environment.

CHAPTER 8
FOUR YARD LESSONS

Level four prison yards made me value freedom and understand jail-house politics. Some of these youngsters do not understand what respecting the next individual really means and need to start off in a level four yard instead of a soft one yard when sentence to prison. Level four prison life is a world of its own that many will never understand, unless they experienced it for themselves. You can view all the movies, documentaries, books, but never really understand how it functions unless you've walked the yard. In your mind, you must be willing to give up your release date on a four-yard because survival is of the essence. Enjoy living, but value freedom—I had to tell myself. It only takes one mistake to lose what we value the most in life. It does not matter your age, ethnicity, or gender—the system will never run out of funds and start releasing level four inmates, as private prisons are now being operated throughout our states. Being in a cell 24 hour a day for months opened my mind to see so many visions that I wanted to see become realities. I had to trust my instincts and learning.

When I was placed on the bus headed back to L.A. County jail to face charges of murder, I knew that I would come back to the same prison with a different mindset. Either I would return with so much anger and be willing to assault the first individual that said the wrong word, including staff, or I was going to come back as humble as possible and finish my term so that I could be an asset to society. Though I still had seven years of prison life that I had to deal with, I tried to keep my mind occupied on positive thoughts and hold on to a release date. I was grateful to have had someone in my life that was uplifting through her beautiful words and sincerity through my trials, even if it were through letters and conversations. I told myself that I would never return to a place where there is no trust amongst anyone— a place that is built for individuals with malice in their hearts. If I ever did return to prison, it would be to speak with my brothers that are fighting and holding on to faith! Without faith, many tend to give up and turn to drugs or get involved in jail-house politics. My utmost respects are for the men in prison that have truly come to value freedom. I know when it is their day to be set free, those who really want to keep their freedom, will be able to do so. Life on the outside is not easy, but it is still easy to remain free. Prison can either be a wakeup call or a place where one can grow old very quickly. For others, prison can be a scapegoat when they have burned their bridges with family and friends.

There are a lot of individuals who are involved in gangs today or say they are about that "life"! I just hope they understand the consequences and are prepared to deal with them. Freedom is a precious gift. If you are gang-banging today and you do not want to stop and make a positive change in your life, then don't mislead the youngsters growing up in the neighborhood. We should be uplifting and encouraging our youth because we already know the consequences of our wrongdoings. No one can make an individual change, other than the individual themselves when they are ready to do so—but incarceration is wasted time and they are not promised to have their freedom ever again. A life sentence in prison isn't worth the streets you fight for, as the streets will forget about you. I believe God has blessed me when at times I wondered why? No matter how dark the day may be, I think of the worst times of my life and God reveals his answer to my question. I can be in a level four yard inside of a six by nine cell for the rest of my life, surrounded by lost souls and becoming one myself, or I can be alive, free, and grateful for every blessing. I do not know what God has in store for me, but I do know he believes in me and is allowing a man who should be dead or in prison with a life sentence have another opportunity to be an asset. What I do with this opportunity is up to me and I know there is no Margin for error, no excuses.

I make no excuses and believe that the only way to survive in a world that will swallow you up like quicksand is to not fall for negative temptation and be patient. The passion I have discovered is to reach our youth through personal testimony and get involved in programs that encourages them to stay positive and hungry to succeed. I gave my word to God through prayer that I would do my part to give awareness to our youth so that they have an opportunity to a positive future. I have always believed in God. Faith and prayer are powerful. During those 12 years inside, I used to ask repeated offenders returning to prison on violations or minor infractions how was life on the "outside," as I called it, and the majority would say that there were no jobs available, the police are always harassing them, and that's how it is in their neighborhood. Many individuals parole to the same environment and continue to associate with gang members they call their "homeboys." I would see men go home and see them return again a few years later, as I was serving my term. It was like a getaway for them as parole violations could only hold them for months. The choice is on every individual on parole to give the state back their number and begin living a free life or continue thinking prison is a luxury resort for men.

As ironic as this may sound, but I believe that prison was the best college I could have ever attended. I was at a point in my life where my actions had profound consequences. I was not setting a good example for my son and getting involved in a life of deeper crime. I also learned how the life I was living before my incarceration was a life full of hate, anger, and without meaning. It took some time to let go of my anger and to begin to appreciate life, even if it would be inside of prison. I had time to reflect on the direction my life was going. I knew that if I did not prepare my own road map, then I would return to prison or be dead in five years. The anger I had inside me from the loss of my father blinded my visions to make negative choices that had severe consequences behind them. I regained my vision through the lessons of the four yards with freedom as the centerpiece.

CHAPTER 9

FREEDOM 07

I recall being in the hole a few months before my release date with time to think about freedom. After all that I had gone through with the trials and losing my release date, I would have cherished that date a bit more, but I was hustling. I stayed in the hole for 90 days until the investigation was over and placed back to general population with less than four months before my schedule release date. I was done with hustling, and I had begun to mentally prepare myself. I started exercising and staying busy with my thoughts. For the next few months, I took the house porter job cleaning up the bathrooms and showers, mopping floors, and taking pride doing so, because if I could do it inside making $20 a month, then I could do it in the free world to survive. I knew that I was going to be a 33-year-old starting at the bottom with nothing in the bank and that I could not be residing in someone's home and not contributing as a responsible adult. The hustler in me was trying to make money to send out so I could have stacked up because $200 that the state was giving me was not going to last. One of my boys had a good plug inside that would bring in tobacco and we would distribute the full can for mail outs. Once tobacco was prohibited throughout the state prisons, there was always guards or free staff who would be willing to bring it in and confide in one inmate to distribute. Although our prison system officials say that only the visitors bring in contraband, but staff and guards have been caught before throughout the system and forced to resign or arrested because of their actions. Cell phones have taken over the market inside now, and I can assure you visitors are not wrapping them up and "keestering" as Will was schooled on "Get Hard."

I could not understand during the time I was inside why a correctional officer was willing to risk their career, income, and freedom, but the root of all evil has a mind of its own that allows us to see problems being solved. From the outside, I can understand the motive for a person earning 100 thousand a year with overtime and excellent benefits to jeopardize their job. The cost of living can be stressful because of the trends people follow, the size of their family, or even personal expenses. Whatever the reason was for the officer involved to risk his job, others will continue to do the same because the cash money is so good.

I still couldn't believe my release date was approaching in two weeks. For years, I would imagine hearing my name being called out on the PA system to pick up my *S-time   slip when names would be called daily it seemed. I had two weeks to turn in all state clothing—which I had no problem doing—and to get my affairs in order. I would walk around the track everyday morning and night alone envisioning my first 30 days out. Doing a set of 25 push up in front of every building around the track to keep up with the goal count. There were no prerelease programs to attend due to budget cuts to prepare for re-entry to society, but here is the main ingredient needed to make it and be mentally strong. If you do not have your mind in a positive direction, you will be a statistic and may not get another opportunity with your freedom. Let's not forget about the "Three Strike Law" that will confine you again for a very long time no matter if it's a violent or nonviolent crime. This law had good intentions, but it took men and women away from their families for many years for wobbler cases or misdemeanors. My brother was a victim to this law and has spent the last 17 years in prison for a case that many would have only received probation on today. His prior convictions that he plead guilty to when he was younger came back to bite him, especially since he took plea bargains on charges that he was honestly innocent. It is better to pick up a lunch box and grind than to play with your third strike.

Two weeks went by so fast that as excited as I was, I was numb once again. I could not believe this was really happening after all these years, and I couldn't believe it until I was out on the other side of the electric fence. I had changed into my dress outs and finger-printed out to be cleared from any warrants and was being trans-ported to the parking lot as my son and nephews were waiting for me. I was given an envelope with $200 gate money and was wished, "good luck." I knew this money was not going to last me a day as I now had to pay for my meals and any other commodities I wanted. On our way home, we stop and had morning breakfast and caught up with the young men that I left as kids. As we ate our meals and headed back home, we were pulled over by the police for speeding; encountering police contact that could have been a parole violation if anything was found inside the car. My nephew was given a ticket, but we were free to go ahead. Ticket cost him some money…I haven't forgotten I promise.

My first night out was perfect spending time with family, eat-ing chicken and pizza all the while thanking God for it all. I was also excited about a very special lady friend that for the past seven years of my incarceration spoiled me with letters and conversation. She was understanding that my first night of freedom had to be spent with my family. We made plans that she would be picking me up after seeing my parole agent the next day. The moment I first saw her was the next day after being released and she looked beautiful. She had a black dress on with a petite body, and she looked so gorgeous. As we were walking toward one another, there was a retired parole office in the center of our path who started talking to us about love. He told us to love each other and be happy. It was weird, but as I look back now, he saw something that shined in us.

*S-Time Slip- (a slip you receive when your release date is in 2-weeks to turn in all state property)

CHAPTER 10
TIPS 2 STAY FREE

I understood finding a job with a felony was not going to be easy, but I was thankful for having a job lined up and a place to live. Though it was not a job that I knew I would make a career out of, at least it was something to help me earn funds so I could feel a part of society. As an ex-felon who was doing the best he could to adapt, I had to learn very quickly to deal with discrimination and how not to get discouraged by it. I had encounter situations that I just wanted to take someone outside and really have a talk with them but being an ex-felon on parole I could have won the physical battle but would have lost the freedom that I value. People are quick to dial "911" and press charges. I have learned to defeat negativity with positive intelligence, remembering to stay on course. I would be lying if I told you everything has been gravy. Not the case. Anytime the "Do not Give A Frank" attitude tried to hit me, I remember all the drama during my incarnation. I immediately had to change my perception, because I had no margin for error. No one wants to be locked in a cage or cell for the rest of their lives, especially after getting a taste of freedom with unlimited possibilities. We are all on the same playing field and can succeed, but we must play by the rules in order to win.

To all the individuals inside correctional institutions serving time that awaits their freedom: begin to educate yourself with the tools that you do have access to like books, college courses, trades, and most importantly time. Be prepared once you go on "S" time knowing that in two weeks your life begins. Without some type of road map, you are bound to become a statistic. I used the word "statistic" a lot because the system has proven that recidivism will continue for those that do not value freedom. The main challenge to make it in a world that one can easily get lost in is "ourselves." We have the patience, especially after serving years inside, now all we need is a positive mentality with drive.

Start speaking with good men who not necessarily are lifers, but that have positive knowledge to share with you. Listen to their voices and if you really listen, you will hear them tell you to become an asset and enjoy your freedom. Enjoy your opportunity of starting over and make an impact somewhere. Many of these rehabilitated men await their opportunity and will be great mentors. My promise to a few lifers before going home was to make it out here. My Native American friend name Noah (Chief) and chess partner told me not to send him anything, he was fine, but to make it out here for him. He was a very humble man with remorse in his heart and great knowledge. There were so many other lifers who I ran across and I appreciated their schooling. They were survivors with a sound mind that did not allow the jail house politics to affect them. Some lifers were innocent and have spent over 20 years in prison for a crime they did not commit, hanging on to hope and not giving up. Recently a lifer I was housed with was release after being incarcerated for 27 years and now declared to be innocent by the Sherriff's Department. For some reason God has allowed for individuals to be incarcerated for a purpose even if they were innocent. It is what you do with your opportunity of freedom.

As a free individual who has passed through the system, I am truly grateful for the lessons of life that I had to encounter. I push for all the lifers and ex-felons who are making a positive difference to give rehabilitated men and women hope upon their freedom. If you are tired of coming back and forth or this was your first time and you never want to return, be real with yourself, be honest with people, and give the same respect that you must give every man inside. Some people out here do not understand respect and can be difficult to deal with, but you must bite your tongue and not allow them to ruin your day.

If you have family and friends support, start asking if anyone they know is hiring. Write down top 10 things that need to get done ASAP! I will help with a few.

- Be with Fam-Bam or positive friends

Eat whatever meal you like, if you can afford it.

Go see parole officer. See what programs you qualify for that State will fund.

DMV ID card or License startup app.

Get Soc Sec card.

Research internet for jobs and resume. You must dedicate your energy for this. Create email account

Buy a bus pass or get a free bus pass if possible. There is no excuse why you cannot make a job interview.

These are just some examples that helped me my first week out.

You have time to sit on your rack and create a road map of your first year out, and your top 10 priorities upon your release. If a family member or friend does help you with a job, then do not let them down. Learn how to adapt with society and let your positive attitude shine. Life is good...when filling out job applications the first thing that HR departments and hiring mangers look at is the "have you ever been convicted" box. It is my favorite box because I see it as an opportunity to sell myself and land the job. I have always answer honestly on application, writing "open," which means, you are willing to discuss. If you sell yourself honestly and are willing to show your employer that there is no other better for the job than you, you may get that shot. Be up front and let the person who is interviewing know you are an ex-con and on parole. If you lie, those are grounds to get fired on. Don't complain about the minimum wage salary, it beats the .10 cent an hour you were getting inside. The real key point here is that you get your parole officer in good terms with you, and your making legal hustle. If the funds aren't enough, then get two jobs or take a trade.

Look at it this way in a sports analogy. You are an undrafted rookie who is getting one chance to prove yourself and earn a contract on a team. The team is a company you are applying with, and you will get your shot to be a part of, but eyes will be viewing you and you must earn trust and respect. You need to be reliable, team player, on time, and have a positive mindset and your hard work will not go unnoticed. After the fifth year, if you are still employed through the same employer and your hard work and loyalty to a company is not appreciated, not valued, then this should be your free agency year. You may have other offers, or you may want to start something up yourself. Let your entrepreneur spirt guide you, as there are endless ways to make a good and honest living. Keep pushing for brighter futures. Research is critical on your end to find out what grants are available for you if you need them. Learning needs energy and you must be willing to put out that energy. Stay hungry and keep pushing toward your goals. Keeping a steady job with a home address where you live in is a recipe for an early parole discharge. That was my number one main goal...discharging! I wasn't a number anymore and was a legal part of society.

Inspire others through your own struggles in life, as you have firsthand experience with life inside of a world that is full of hatred, emotional pain, and isolation. If we can help one youngster who is willing to listen to some positive and realistic advice, then we can strengthen our communities. My goal with this book is to encourage all individuals, including ex-felons to understand their value. We must be willing and ready to contribute to society fighting through the struggles to reach our daily goals. There is reward beyond measurements from speaking to our youth that outweighs monetary donations. When I get someone, who approaches me after the event to thank me for something I said, it gives me motivation to continue through my journey.

Vacation time is over once those gates open. We must face reality, and the reality as it was for me was that $200 gate money was not going to last me one night if I had nowhere to go. Not everyone has the family support that I had, but do not let that be an excuse to fail. There are shelters and programs available if you need help, but you must be willing to accept them until you can get on your feet. Take advantage of everything your parole officer can help with because it is very easy to fall back into the lifestyle of what we know, which if you have or are serving time it is usually something illegal. The rate of recidivism is so high in this country and correctional officers love that because of job security, and we can't be mad at them for that. They are getting paid well to watch grown ass men all day. Leave the "tough guy" role inside—I warn you. Humble yourself and embrace life staying positive understanding that your energy can be contagious. Don't get caught up with the false promises of the street life.

I see there are grown men who do not want to grow up and are encouraging youngsters in negative fashions, because they want to stay young themselves. Some people have a platform to reach out and guide the youth but chose to glamorize the street life. Just because they have money to clown with, they forget what matters most out of life. There is nothing wrong in having money and being successful in which ever field a person has been blessed in, but don't let money control you. One thing money can buy you is false friends and meaningless relationships, possessions that you will lose, and laughs, but what it cannot buy you is freedom! There are many balling out of control in prison having packages and maxed out canteen every month, but top ramens get old after a few meals.

I can respect and understand individuals' action today for wanting money. Opportunities are everywhere, even if the hustle is not legal. As an ex-felon with two strikes, you now understand why there is no margin for error for me, but many youngsters without a record are willing to take penitentiary chances for money—the root of all evil. Jeopardizing your freedom to provide some cushion to your situation is not worth it and you can lose your vision; but it's a game that many will continue to partake in, getting money anyway they can and giving up everybody to avoid jail time nowadays. Notable example from our political leaders and their associates who know they broke the law and now are working with law enforcement to give up everything they know or go to jail. Speaking from experience here, 12 straight years in prison was not worth the 200 thousand that was supposed to be in the home, but keeping my mouth shut and dealing with my consequences for 12 years was the only way out. I was young with a negative come up mind frame and needed the lesson that was coming my way to slow my roll. My partner in crime has now passed away because of medical reasons, but never had to question my loyalty with his freedom.

If you want to dabble in old come ups, then be willing to deal with the consequences all over again. I was at a point where I thought about dabbling at the beginning, but the feeling I had inside my stomach and dealing with new face individuals just didn't feel right. I felt like when I was sent to CMC-East from reception center. The first day I was there, I knew I had to get out of this place and quickly. Went inside the chow hall and there was metal forks and spoons and no correctional officer accounting for silver ware on your way out. It was like take one and have your cell tossed up minutes later and being escorted to the hole. I'm sure you understand my language but if you didn't, there was a whole lot of dry snitching going on. Not everyone in the game is with it—but the streets are the same in that aspect where individuals want to play the game, but don't want to respect the code. Quick to work out deals to avoid prison giving up their connections and continue to front as the plug. Transform your hustle into a legal way, not looking back and shaking off anyone who is not supporting or pushing with you. Not everyone in the game is going out backwards and singing like a trump team, but there is no margin for error. Do not let negativity minds steer us in directions that we have experience already but use your own mind to determine how and where you want your future to be. Focus and keep it pushing!

CHAPTER 11
DEFEATING THE ODDS

My reasons to defeat the odds are plenty. To name a few: family, friends, and genuine love from the one who invested so many years believing in a dream are my main reasons but waking up to freedom is what gives me the motivation to make something productive happen. Defeating the odds applies to all who have experience hardships through their upbringings, who have made wise decisions to grind and enjoy what life has to offer. I can assure you that not every day has been great, but every day has been a blessing. I tip my hat to all that have made mistakes and have grown from that experience. Remaining free today and living a productive positive lifestyle, making an impact somewhere and in someone's life. Adapting to the free world wasn't simple, as there were obstacles that challenged me to consider choices that seemed right, that weren't actually right. I was homeless and living out of my car for days at a time, but I was grateful for not being inside of a prison cell, appreciating that I had a car to sleep in for the moment and finding ways to survive legally. I had the choice to hit the streets and hustle, make a few bucks jeopardizing my freedom and feeling sorry for myself, but after having a small taste of freedom, I wasn't going to give it back. I chose my car and God has blessed me every time to continue and enjoy life. I already knew my consequences, and that is a life sentence. Everyone has flaws, but you must catch yourself and direct the course you want your path to go. Patience is truly a virtue, which will reward you with your needs.

I have ups and downs, but through prayer and guidance, I have been blessed with 10 years of freedom, and I am loving every moment. Pushing to write an ending that will leave a positive print. Today, I chose to live a life that I am content with, giving back to our youths through projects they can relate with and accepting every invitation to speak when it comes to reaching our youth. I understand the importance of responsibility. Within the first year of regaining my freedom, I was in awe witnessing a single parent of two young teens getting up daily to manage and provide a roof, clothing, and food for her household. She was not jeopardizing her family by cutting corners to overcome the struggle or just lying around complaining about life. This woman was my rock, my strength, and my confidant during the most challenging time of my life. Her drive inspired me to fight with her to achieve the comfort of living and working together as a team to assure bills were paid. Having a good partner is key to stay on a positive path, but good friendships and having a job are very important also.

My plea to all my nieces and nephews is to continue and push forward towards their visions. Struggling is part of the process to discover our passion and never forget the struggle of life to appreciate the freedom we have. You do not come from a breed without drive, but a bloodline with ambition. We all can win but we must put heart into it. Seeing some of you graduate from college and serving our country fills me with pride. Take advantage of the opportunities for fighting for our country and enjoy the beauty of life the way you choose to. You must want to be a part of society and appreciate freedom as a true blessing.

I have found a woman who truly loves and respects me, which I embrace gracefully. During my years inside, I fell in love with the beautiful spirt of my wife. Although her physicality is extremely attractive, it is her loyalty that I find priceless. A partner will help you value your freedom enough to get up daily and grind to enjoy those blessings. Women can be our backbone to success without a doubt. It could be your mother, sister, or that special woman who displays her beauty. Not everyone gets an opportunity to endure true freedom again, so let us live free with joy, love, and do our best to give the next individual an opportunity to be given another chance through your success story. Individuals can change once they learn to value life and appreciate freedom. You must not allow situations to get the best of you and be in control to find a solution to any problem. You will meet some of the same obstacles that I ran across and they will challenge you, but I have given you the formula. The moral to all this is that, it is up to you to appreciate the ability to walk into mall and just thank God for giving you a second chance, even if you are just window shopping—you are at least free to appreciate life. Youngsters need mentors, and who else would be more suited. Saving one life is worth far more than taking one.

Becoming an asset to society is part of God's plan as he can use our personal story to inspire others to make an about face and really focus on the direction our lives are headed at the time. If you truly want to change your story, you must have a vision of growth. My story is simple, just like my life is today. I work and have flexibility with my schedule, which helps me line up speaking engagements at schools or juvenile halls whenever I am given the opportunity. As a rehabilitated ex-felon, it is my job to accept opportunities to reach out to our youth whenever asked by counselors or organizations that work with them. I believe in reaching out to our youth before they make some of the same mistakes that have proven to cause failures, setbacks, and lost time with love ones. Not all the youth I speak with will get the message of how much of a blessing it is to be free! But my promise to God is to reach the ones we can through my story and the stories of others that are defeating the odds by becoming assets to society. We can all make a positive impact or continue to play the game and accept the consequences from the risk we take. Speaking with the youth has been a blessing and priceless. This may not be for you once you are free, but just making it out here and contributing to society a positive vibe, you too can help break the cycle. There are so many organizations that are working to improve lives—if you see yourself making a difference, then you must join them. Believe it when I say that everyone can be an asset to society in their own way. Keep a humble heart and reach people. The higher you go in life, always make a path so the next individual that is hungry can have an outlet. My passion for our youth will continue to grow with visions of building a team of many men and women who have made mistakes in their lives and now take the time to speak with a sincere heart to our youngsters.

CHAPTER 12
A HEAVY LOST

I have experienced 10 years of freedom now and I want to thank so many people who have helped guide me with their words, support, and trust. I have learned so much, and I truly appreciate their love—from family, friends, co-workers, and bosses. I have experienced some high points during these years of freedom, but I have also been faced with some low points. Some of those low points were losing my hunger to win after the loss of my mother and moving on from the woman I once envisioned as my wife. After my first 3 years of freedom, I decided to move on in a different direction. I engaged in a new relationship with another woman for seven years after letting go of my true love. I was settling going to work and coming back home to a relationship that was more like a roommate arrangement. I had lost my drive and was contemplating moving on alone without any destination in mind. I did not see marriage or starting a family with the woman I was involved with and lost interest in her due to her insecurities. Before my mother died, she was in a medical rehabilitation center recovering from what I believe was a weak heart. She mentioned to me during a visit with her that she understood what my brother and I felt like not having freedom. She felt incarcerated and not her free self whom she was for so many years after losing my father. She was forced to stay at the center for two weeks needing a doctor to sign off before releasing her to freedom again. My mother did not want any more hospital stays, medications, or treatments; all she wanted was to enjoy her last days on this earth. I was upset with her for not saying goodbye when she knew that not taking her medication and not doing what the doctor ordered since it would lead to her death. My queen, my mother, was tired and ready to rest with her husband who was brutally murder 25 years ago. A month after being release from the center, she died. On August 5th, 2015 I was awakened just before midnight with a voice in my ear informing me that my mother just died. I knew this would be coming, but not this soon. Within a few hours, my siblings and family were on the road driving in three cars 18 hours to lay her to rest. My mother wanted to die in Mexico because she wanted to be buried at the same plot my father was in. She made my sisters promise her that if she died in the U.S. we would have to figure it out and ship her body to Mexico as my father's body was in 1991.

After sending off our mother the way she requested, with music, respect, and love, we returned home to everyday life. I had contemplated moving on from the life and the relationship I was involved in and starting fresh someplace else—it did not matter what state. Timing was not right to move out or move on. I continued to work and carry my weight until I was ready to fight again for the dreams I once had. I invested two more years in this nonchalant relationship with nothing growing but us apart. I knew that something was missing in my life and needed to make a move and fast. Being accused of infidelities constantly was getting old and a change was coming.

I decided after speaking with my live-in girlfriend—whatever we were that it was time—to leave. We had gone through this same argument before and every time we would work things out after a few days, but I knew it would have to be a decisive decision. We were on two different standpoints and she had major trust issues that started way before I was in the picture. Seven years and no growth, so without any blueprints I gathered few things that I could fit in my car, headed on the I-15 and did not look back. I drove out to Vegas with no plans and was approved for an apartment that day. The moment I was approved, a huge weight lifted off my shoulders. I was not worried about furniture or anything; I had a place of my own that I could relax and not live in a household with tension. Work was secure, but I was willing to let that go and start fresh somewhere else or get creative and push hard to earn a living. I was a 42-year-old man with a passion to reach our youth and letting my vision sleep. Living in Vegas helped me gather my thoughts as I was dealing with closing out accounts I had for work. As a young hustler all my life, Vegas was also a test to myself to remain on focus and be in control of my gambling habits. I wasn't moving out there to gamble and get caught up in a lifestyle that I knew would be addictive if I chose to partake in. I needed alone time to focus and contemplate my next moves. Staying up late until the morning hours writing and working on my passion again and feeling excited about life. Bills began to pile up, and I needed to get back to work or figure it out. Praying not to lose sight of hope and fall into negative temptation.

During this time, a blessing from above with my mother's touch re-enters into my life and I knew that I could not lose my "beauty" ever again. I am grateful for her love and her sincere heart. She had been a true loyal friend that never gave up on us even as I decided to move on elsewhere. She respected the relationship that I was involved in for years, without interfering and raising her two young teenagers respectfully. When we tried to build more than just our friendship upon my release from prison, I ruined our chances by not allowing our relationship to flourish due to my lack for understanding relationships. I had the mentality of not allowing her to question me and learning adapting to society. I wasn't looking for the grass to be greener anywhere else, I just did not want to hurt her and her kids any further by arguing with their mom every day as I was trying to learn about life. The kids were at an age where seeing their mother not happy and crying constantly could have had a negative effect on their goals, so I decided to move on.

As the years went by, I would be accused of being in contact with her on a weekly basis. I didn't know much about her life now since I had my own relationship, but I always prayed that she was happy and enjoying her life. Through the transitions of my life, I struck gold...and knew I had to put a ring on it.

The high points in my life have been marrying the person who I always imagined throughout the years of incarceration. Keeping my freedom for 10 years, understanding and adapting to society, and building meaningful relationships. Speaking to our youth in juvenile camps, schools, and on the streets, even if it is a keep it pushing message. Being a part of creating a t-shirt entrepreneur workshop has opened my visions wider to deliver a message of hope and motivation. Working with our youth can be challenging as they are easily enticed to the glamour of the street life, but there is always that one that can be reached. A man is only as good as his word, and the only one I owe mine to is God.

I am blessed daily with a morning text and sometimes even twice a day from a very special lady who uplifted me with her love for God and her reliable attributes. She ministers through text messages, uplifting and encouraging many and loves her church family. Her spiritual quotes and words are always on target. She has a beautiful spirt and a smile so bright that you can feel her positive energy the moment you see her. I am grateful for people in my life that are positive in spirit with a genuine heart.

I have a great Pastor friend who is fully devote to God and productive in our communities that I can speak with, and I know I will get the correct advice from when needed. The church and men's groups that he has invited me to have always taught me that God is always there for us. I really enjoyed different views of men who fear and love God and do their best to live a positive lifestyle. Men that value their marriages and relationships and are willing to help one another out through meaningful and respectable conversation. Grown men giving positive tips and vibes that help us grow together as men. Ten years is what I gave myself to fully feel like I could understand how to adapt to a fast-past world and become an asset to society. I am grateful for all the relationships as mention before, but truly grateful to God. I pray every day to value the beauty of life and to create the memories that we all will leave behind. I also pray for all the good lifers who gave me nothing but positive words throughout my education from the State of California's hard knocks. Their words to be grateful that I had a release date guided me during uncertain moments.

Keeping my promise to God has given me blessing after blessing. Life is full of riches and not all are made from trees. I have learned that if you do things from the heart and with God's guidance, the rewards are joy, love, understanding, and freedom. If I have learned anything from the trials that decided where I am today, they have taught me to grow as a person with dignity, respect, and class. I have definitely made mistakes through these 10 years, but mistakes that one has grown from stronger.

Hats off to those who have succeeded in their careers or business ventures being raised in rampant gang environments and are making an impact in their communities. Giving our young ones hope that success can be attain by anyone willing to put in the work. We are in a pivotal time of cultural change and it is up to the generation of the 80's and 90's to reach our youth and give them positive game as they are our future to the generations to come.

I see unity in many communities' standing together for positive changes and on natural disasters that makes me proud of being a part of a great country. So many blessed individuals are giving back from their hearts and that makes a person want to be a part of life. The new chase now is to follow my passion and God will provide what is needed. A new business venture awaits to open, with goals of reaching the youth that want to grow in a positive direction. Speaking with our youth is my true passion and God continues to pour in innovative ideas to grow a team that will make an impact. Giving up is not option as strength to overcome all situations we all have in us. I meant every word of that prayer in the holding tank during my trial and appreciate what God has provided throughout these 10 years of freedom.

My prayer now is to grow our network of speakers and workshops so that we can motivate people and avoid school shootings through the powerful message of our speakers. As the journey begins to reach our youth, I encourage everyone that has a success story to share with our youth their motivation to succeed. Your knowledge of survival, patience, and costly mistakes can uplift the youth. Many of us are on borrowed time, and it's time to pay it forward. The grind for me is to reach them, thinking outside of the box to grab their attention and focus on where they want to head in life. Spitting street knowledge and building trust amongst each youngster we encounter with positive motivation. I have been grateful for the opportunity to work with students and learn so much from them and appreciate the attention and respect they give me for my time. Their show of appreciation is what keeps me hungry to give back to our youth hoping to steer them away from negative affiliations and present them with opportunities. This is my grind. If I am blessed with life, then I will walk through any doors that welcomes my passion. We live in a world that has doors open for success, and if you are not willing to walk through them all to find you're a passion, then you are settling for less.

Working in sales for the last 10 years, I have met bright individuals in businesses that have shared valuable tips to their success. They remain humble with great wealth. The same wealth is attainable for us all, but our passion and hunger must be on point. I am blessed to have a job that supports my vision with a positive team that grinds hard. I have a woman in my life who I appreciate and respect. Life is beautiful and though it is not sunny daily, we must make it a reason to see sunshine in every day. What I have today is priceless with an unobstructed vision to push toward a mission. This grind will produce a chain of change, that men and women will make an impact through their stories.

My utmost respects go out to all the men and women who serve on our armed forces that give so many the liberties to enjoy whatever it is we choose to do. Yes, even us ex-cons, our troops fight for us too. I missed out with joining the service as I was incarcerated when my mother told me I had received a letter to join. It would have been an honor to serve for freedom.

I thank everyone for their time in reading this book and with a message to pass a positive vibe along to someone daily. If it be at a coffee shop, or at work, it really makes a person's day. I commend all ex-felons that were incarcerated and now are living productive lives. Being assets to their families and contributing in dropping the recidivism rate from their positive contributions to society. Never stop pushing, my brothers, because of the failures in the past, but rather push harder for the visions of your future. Prisons will never be torn down due to lack of funding. This is a billion-dollar business operated through our federal government that will welcome each ex-felon back with open arms. Let's be a part of a movement that helps keep our youth out of these prisons through sharing your message to them. I have achieved my goals of discharging my parole, breathing free fresh air, and reaching our youth.

CHAPTER 13

REACH N THE NEXT 1

For the past few years, I have made it my mission to help youth by sharing personal experiences of prison and life. Every teen needs direction towards their path and schools are looking for help from individuals and organizations that can reach these teens and motivating them to achieve their goals.

Through the support of counselors and teachers in local schools and with the help of passionate hearts for our youth, a project has been created to spend time with teens inside of their schools and present them with a tee shirt development project. The goal is to speak with the youth sharing personal experiences to help change a negative thought or action into a positive outcome. Our team bonds and motivates them through the stories of others they can relate with. The speakers who come in have defeated adversity in their lives and now share their success stories to encourage others.

The pilot programs were successful with overwhelmed feelings of joy from the letters of appreciation from students wrote to me after the project was completed. Those letters inspired me to continue and be a part of projects that will reach other youth throughout cities everywhere, creating opportunities. I have seen before my own eyes the effects of this program on our youth, and I hope to network with others that share the same visions. Traveling to speak is a blessing as I see sights that so many takes for granted. It is time to bring "Reach N the Next 1 Project" to life starting off where it all started. My troubled years started during the first year of Hamilton Middle School, because I was suspended and finally expelled. I cheated myself in many ways of succeeding in a place that offered opportunities. The only view I wanted to have was the street hustle that gave me a high by making money. I did not appreciate school enough to give myself a chance with a baseball scholarship, even if I was the only one that saw that vision in my head. Time and energy were not dedicated in understanding that a scholarship was a tool to use in finding my itch. Playing in local baseball leagues would keep me away from the streets as much as possible and even made my high school team but was let go from the team due to my grades below "C" average.

Remembering the past can be guide in creating our future. A team is being gathered to produce a workshop with clarity, and motivational. A team of powerful speakers with remarkable success stories with a sincere heart. I do not recall many speakers coming to our middle school and speak with us regarding similar programs from my school days, but if there were, I was one of the teens that just had to experience what was to come. I see so many motivational speakers today uplifting many through their stories of success and that is my view of reaching the next one project. We can inspire and be inspired through paths that others have walked in order to gain appreciation for life.

It is an honor to have the opportunity in returning to my home school 20 plus years later to present opening a project conceived thinking outside of the box. I asked only for one shot from all who support the goals described throughout this book, and thankful for the trust and confidence with your endorsements. The task is not over as there is so much more, we can be a part of. So, let's push, and push daily. We have no margin for error.

CHAPTER 14
FREEDOM IS LIVING

As I sit here and write this concluding chapter, I sit on a beach with white sands and clear blue waters in Hawaii. I am touring the North Shore and witnessing the tropical weather. A blessed man married to the woman I pictured in my mind for many years, enjoying the memories that we promised to create on paper. The words that were written in letters were feelings that were strongly meant as I was thankful for a friendship that was uplifting. It was because of a sudden change in both of our lives, but the timing so perfect that it made our fairytale love story into a reality. Following our hearts to share the blessings that God has in line for us, moving forward to achieve visions that were only that at a time. I wear my ring with pride representing the love and respect I have for my wife.

Through the years apart, I learned that if you are not with the right person, who trusts and believes in you, then you will be unhappy and your hunger to strive will be dull. I found myself in this dilemma for years until I was willing to move on and let that person go no matter how much time was invested with them and wish them well. God allows for us to make decisions that we can learn and grow from and when to walk away. My heart is at ease in the direction it is headed and the companion it is headed with. There are so many ways to interpret freedom, but mine is simple. Being able to go without handcuffs or shackles and having the freedom to enjoy a day of whatever it is, or wherever it may be is what I call freedom.

I made my fair mistakes in life, but the best part of them is that they have taught me to grow. To mature into a man that understands his path, and not letting my father's death be in vain. Crossing paths with my wife was the push I was looking for, as she was my missing piece to the puzzle we started together when we were just teenagers.

Road trips are the best, as I am now free to stretch my legs or kick them up on a dashboard, listening to music with the window down or A.C. blowing. I put two fingers in the air at every State Prison bus on the highways as a sign to keep pushing to those inside being transferred to a correctional facility. I give God thanks for taking me off that bus and in the company of a beautiful woman who helps guides our destination with her google maps. Every day is a blessing, but the grind is just beginning as there is "No Margin 4 Errors" ...with the utmost respects...

Alfredo Barrios Sr.

This book is dedicated to:

To all the youth that gave me the respect to speak from the heart. Through every event that I have participated in, I have gained a deeper passion to pursue the visions that I contemplated in my mind. I like to thank the school counselors, teachers, and principles that open their doors to allow me to speak to their students and think outside of the box with workshops.

To Rick Coffman, a friend and mentor through my flag football days as a kid. Thank you for your help with opening doors inside the juvenile system and a partner in "REACH N THE NEXT 1" workshops. For being a mentor to so many youths incarcerated that either will heed your positive message or will have learn in a difficult way.

Thank you to, Simon Anaya and the entire Anaya team, for their time and sincere assistance in teaching the printing section to students and with printing tee shirts with them. Sincere hearts have a winning team.

Thank you to Lionel Gonzalez for your trust in me and your passion for the youth. Schools need more LG's. You will always be appreciated by one of your students throughout their journey. I am grateful for your friendship.

To my pastor and friend, Gregory Sanders, who does not give up on me and is a blessing to so many. To Gloria, thank you for being so loyal and uplifting daily. The scriptures you send every day are always on point. God places certain people in our lives to keep us on track, and I am grateful for your sincere love. To Carrie (Mom) I like to thank you for "Awake & Watch Tower" magazines during my years of being lost. There are so many religious beliefs, but all have one God—for your letters and pictures of my son as he was growing up. Thank you for everything, and for encouraging me to pursue speaking with our youth today. I love you...

To my son Alfredo Jr: I failed you and I know it. Jeopardizing my freedom was not all I gave up, as I gave up the opportunity to watch you grow and share all the moments that a father should be a part of. I am sorry for that and no excuse can justify the risk I took. The only honest answer I have is that I was immature following the wrong hustle without thinking about the outcome. I am proud of you for understanding your mistakes and for recognizing your purpose to push. No matter how difficult your road ahead looks, you can get through as long as you understand your purpose. God blessed you with a beautiful daughter for a reason. Do not make the same error as I did, jeopardizing your future not being around for your daughter. Grind as much as you have to legally, with my granddaughter as your motivation. You already are such a better father than I was, now it's time to put all your energy into creating a positive future for your family. I do love you, always have, and always will. I do believe that you will find your passion and succeed. The only way you will lose is to give up and make excuses. Keep it pushing Jr.

To my nieces and nephews. I am proud of you all. In every one of you I see a loving heart with goals. Stay hungry and push to reach those goals living your best life. I love you all no matter the distance in our relationships.

To my brothers and sisters, Tony, Mike, Juana, and Inez...we have truly been our brothers' keepers throughout our upbringings.

Overcoming difficult moments in our lives that scared us all in our own way. Always having one another's back and supporting decisions made, even if they were not law abiding. I am proud to have solid brothers and sisters that understood the lifestyle we once participate in made us value life and wanting better for our children. We lost the heads of our household, but their spirits and memories are always with us. I love each one of you and appreciate your support through the ride of the system.

To my brother in-law Richard (RIP) you were always our brother and will never be forgotten in our hearts.

To my family and friends, mentors, and everyone that I have had the pleasure to grow from mentally and has encourage me; Thank you! To all the individuals that took time to read this book and helped support another workshop in some school or juvenile hall; Thank you!

To my best men Anthony & Rene. Thank you both for always keeping me focus and respecting my path. For giving me the advice of a true friend during the stressful moments. I appreciate the vote of confidence and the loyalty. A man is truly rich when he has friends that he can call a "FRIEND".

To my beautiful wife Jessica Ann Barrios…our paths crossed at a very young age with googly eyes of puppy love. Though we never pursued the teen boyfriend or girlfriend labels, we felt something special in our hearts. Your beauty always stood out as your smile and soft girlish voice had me wanting to see more of you, but my immaturity did not allow for me to be a gentleman at the time. Throughout the years, I would hear you were in town and my heart would pump harder than usual from the thought in running into you. As our paths finally crossed, we could only converse through a recorded line and letters that developed into a platonic friendship, with sincere feelings. You stood by me and fought through the most difficult times of my life, inspiring me to hold on to faith. You gave me a different view of freedom sharing with me the simplicity of happiness with someone to share your life with.

I am truly grateful for your friendship, your uplifting words through your letters, and your sincere love. We have fulfilled a vision we both shared together as husband and wife. Though our path to get here had roadblocks, our love for each other was always in our hearts. Thank you for your support with this book and all my crazy ideas that time was spent on. I will fight to keep you smiling and loving you throughout my days. The fairytale that seemed just that, is now a reality to create meaningful memories. We are a team that feeds from one another and stays motivated and thankful for our blessings. There are many more blessings to be a part of and I look forward in sharing them all with you. I Love You My Beauty & appreciate you entirely.

Finally, I like to thank God for being by my side every day during my worst times. He listens to my cries, to my wants, and to my needs. He provided the last chance to live a life of freedom and to pass his blessings onto others. I'm grateful for my freedom, giving God the praise on a daily basis. Thank You, Lord.

NO MARGIN 4 ERROR IS DEDICATED TO THE MEMORY OF MOM & DAD:

EMMA & BERNARDO BARRIOS (resting together now)

You gave us all you could materialistically and made sure we all had something to eat daily. You taught us to be humble, respect-ful, & grateful, displaying your faithfulness through your daily dedication to get up to grind and provide. Your memories will forever remain in our minds and hearts, pushing daily as you both taught us to do.

Siempre en Mi Corazon...

UNCLE RICH

In Loving Memory of Ricardo Ortiz: A man who kept his word with me and never let me down. You were my mentor, my uncle, and my second father. I miss you every day and will forever keep your memory alive within my heart. Every time I hear "Las Nieves De Enero" playing, I know you are speaking to me. Until we all meet up again...R.I.P.

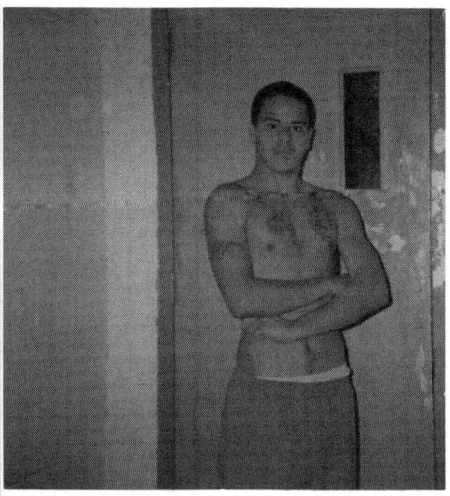

1991 Eastlake JH (Facing 15 yrs to life)

1988-89 $$$ Mindset

1993 State Prison
Chuckawalla

2000-07 in Ca Prison System after the trials. Grateful to have the support of family.